U N S U B

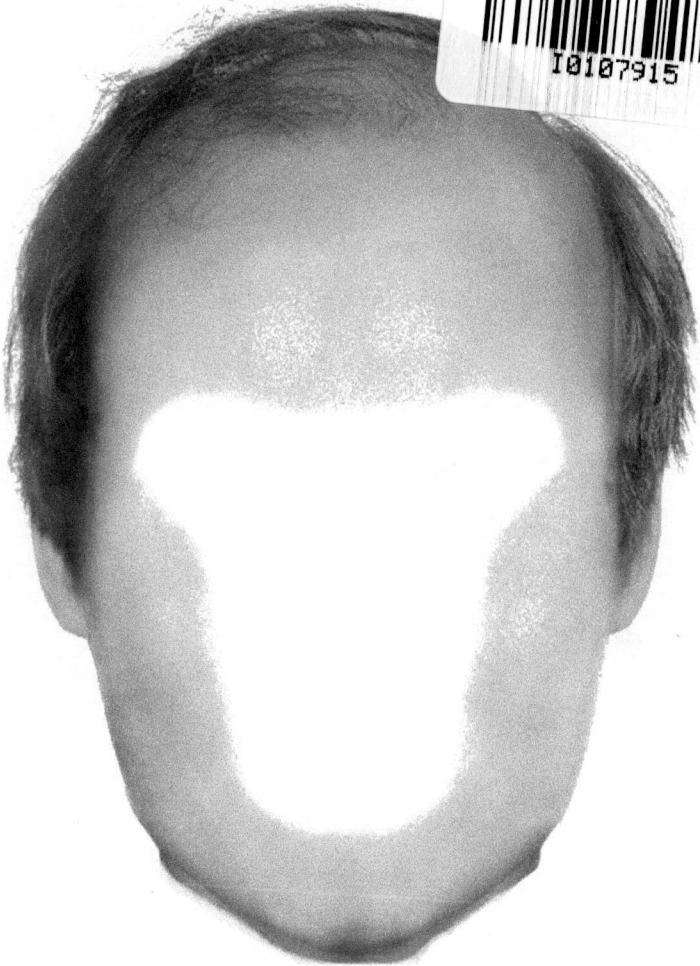

DIVYA VICTOR

UNSUB
Divya Victor
Inert Blanc Press 2015
ISBN: 978-0-9911092-7-2

Cover and title pages designed by Mathew Timmons using art from Brian Joseph Davis' project *The Composites*.

UNSUB

DIVYA VICTOR

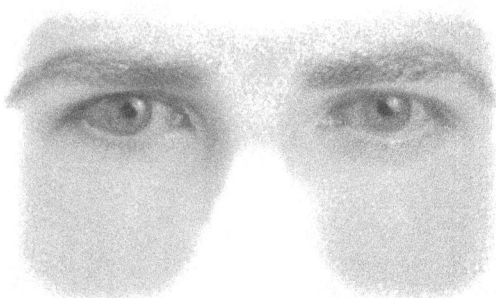

INSERT
BLANC
PRESS
Los Angeles

In the FBI, the unapprehended and unidentified perpetrator of a crime is known as unsub: unknown subject.

high-profile cases
low-risk victims

high-risk lifestyles
flow of profile

high-priority victim
low-profile case

Face-to-face case
briefings

face to face

murder specifies a specific number of murderers

murder does not specify a specific number of victims

prosopopoeia:

In 2 to 3 days discoloration will appear on the skin of my abdomen. My abdomen will begin to swell and fill with gas.

In 3 to 4 days the discoloration will spread and I will look bruised all over. My veins will become dark and visible.

In 5 to 6 days my intestines will swell outward and my skin will be covered in small blisters. My interior will begin to froth and foam.

In 2 weeks my internal pressure will near maximum capacity. Fly eggs will hatch in me and I will fill with maggots. They will live with me and I with them.

In 3 weeks my tissues will have softened. My organs and cavities will collapse and burst. My nails will fall off. My inside will leave me through my openings—my ears, nostrils, anus. Soon, the maggots will migrate and leave me for dead.

In 4 weeks my soft tissue—my arms, my thighs, my cheeks—will liquefy, and my face will become unrecognizable to you.

the development of the individual

1. life experiences

2. certain biological factors

3. heredity

4. upbringing

5. personal choices

part i

$100, 000

a computer "expert"
has demonstrated above-average knowledge regarding computers
has use of the Internet
has the ability to integrate into various socio-economic classes
an expert at social engineering
possesses an educational background conducive to gaining employment
may advertise online as a tutor or male nanny

has a mole under left eye

$100, 000

an avid golfer, snowboarder, skier, and dirt biker
enjoys being the center of attention
has been known to frequent nightclubs
enjoys showing off high-priced vehicles, boats, and other toys
has been described as possibly having bisexual tendencies

speaks fluent French

$100, 000

has reportedly made previous statements
may have plans to kill a police officer
has tattoos of the words "Natalie" and "Cuatro" on left arm
has "Flats" tattooed on right arm
has "In Memory Serelone Flew" and "Flats4" tattooed on back
has a tattoo on chest
has a pierced ear

may have removed tattoos with a laser

$100, 000

speaks fluent Spanish

$100, 000

is physically fit
is an avid outdoorsman, hunter, and fisherman
has a noticeable gold crown on his upper left first bicuspid tooth
known to chew tobacco heavily
may walk with an exaggerated, erect posture and chest pushed out

has surgical scars on lower back

$100, 000

may wear facial hair to include a moustache
known to be a heavy smoker

has pockmarks on face

$100, 000

may have altered fingerprints

has a scar on face

$100, 000

scars on forehead
scars on cheek
scars on back

$100, 000

has a one-inch scar on body
has a mole on shoulder blade

part ii

$5, 000, 000

this alleged member

has a mole on the face

$5, 000, 000

this alleged member

has a chemical burn on the right thigh

$5, 000, 000

this alleged member

wears eyeglasses, a moustache, a beard

$5, 000, 000

this alleged member

speaks with a Yemeni accent and drives taxis

$5, 000, 000

this alleged member

may have facial hair

$5, 000, 000

this alleged member

may have facial birthmarks

$5, 000, 000

this alleged leader

$5, 000, 000

this alleged member

has a receding hairline and a beard

$5, 000, 000

this alleged member

has ties

part iii

_____ *concerning this person*

will be recovered nude
with hands

will be listed
as stab wounds

the distance between
the inside

where s/he
will be known
to engage

where s/he
will be with hands
behind

_____ *concerning this*

_____ *concerning this person*

will slam the head
into the bathroom
floor

and will be told to leave

will dwell in
transitional neighborhoods

_____ *concerning this*

is clean cut
is possibly wearing glasses
is a crack addict
is speaking in the English language
has a possible first name of Vincent

_____ *concerning this person*

will turn the head
to light a cigarette

will turn back
toward the front

subject will press
on the throat

the breast and will tell
calm or s/he

a circle
will be placed over
the head

will cinch the neck
to a seat
to a headrest

_____ *concerning this*

diazepam (valium)
carisoprodol (soma)
omeprazole (stomach antacid)
a loaded .38 caliber revolver
several knives
large white zip ties
camping equipment
binoculars
Tojan-Enz condoms
Gallo wine
Crown Royal
a large industrial black trash bag
his person and vehicle

_____ *concerning this person*

will be held and will
in the early morning hours

and will be held

_____ *concerning this*

a plain, dull-finished wedding band
a black handgun with a chrome slide
a slim build, brown eyes and brown eyebrows
black tactical-style clothing
a mustard-yellow construction hard hat
a reflective vest
a white- or silver-colored 2001-2008 Plymouth
a Chrysler minivan with the rear seats removed

_____ *concerning this person*

will find a body
of another

will survive the wounds

link will lead
another

will wound
again around a face

_____ *concerning this*

a thin moustache
a jaw line beard
a hoop earring in the left ear
a matching mesh basketball shirt
a "widow's peak" hairline
a shirt, light blue in color, with white
stripes on the sides and white edging
has scars
a gold chain with a cross pendant
an accent or use of broken English

markers indicate the depths of tissue to be added to these skulls, how a cast should be applied to the bones. my love, follow in my direction—the direction in which the skin of a human cadaver will split when struck with a spike, don't be a dummy, let me,

> *here, now stretch your*
> *mouth & lips. open your mouth*
> *wide & shut it again &*
> *stretch your lips into*
> *a smile, now pucker up.*

studies over the past century of males and females of different ancestral groups determine the measures of these depths. my love, go deeper into the soft tissue plunging where the thumb presses into the sockets of the mouths, don't be a dummy, let me,

> *here, now when mouthing*
> *words such as beat, bay,*
> *boot, rubber, sober,*
> *rub, job, pick, grasp*
> *keep your lips together &*
> *let the air slide out*
> *of your small gap.*

applying strips of clay, the artist begins to rebuild the faces by filing in around the markers. my love, fill up, fill up a bag with the glasses, and wigs, and glass eyes, and gold chains and the picnics, my love, don't be a dummy, let me,

> *here, now your tongue*
> *needs to be low &*
> *you need to pull it back &*
> *make your mouth go round &*
> *you have to relax the lip*
> *around the socket.*

the artist begins to refine features around these artificial eyes, my love, and the lips take shape to accurately personalize the reconstruction of these remains. don't be a dummy, let me.

the vultures circle
the vultures circle

culture

forensic, *adj.* and *n.*

> < Latin *forensis* (< ***forum*** *n.*) + -*ic suffix.*

forum, *n.*
> < Latin *forum*
>> : as the place of public discussion; hence *fig.*

www.ingramcontent.com/pod-product-compliance
Lightning Source LLC
Chambersburg PA
CBHW051740040426
42447CB00008B/1228